//ALIGNED TIME JOURNAL

Align Your Time
Grow Your Business

If found, please call:

STARTED: _____ /_____ /_____

ENDED: _____ /_____ /_____

Dedicated to my clients, whose towering potential for greatness inspires my work.

You are destined to change the world for the better, and I'm delighted to help.

Amanda

CONTENTS

INTRODUCTION

....

*"Align your time to your deepest intentions, and you will
experience a life of joy, impact, and success."*

—Amanda Crowell

I STARTED OBSESSING ABOUT TIME management when I was an educational consultant supporting public schools in making sustainable change. I loved the work I was doing and I believed in the impact we were making.

I was dedicated to doing it well.

Perfectly, even.

At the same time, I was the mother of two small children, building a coaching practice on weekends, and trying to get my writing published. It was a lot, even before things got crazy.

Working in schools has a very predictable flow. Projects get underway slowly in the fall, pick up speed after Christmas, and reach a fever pitch from March through June. Springtime was no longer about flowers and new beginnings. Instead, Spring was the time when all fourteen of my projects would dramatically intensify at the same time, leaving me feeling inundated and overwhelmed.

Despite my genuine commitment, I found myself on the productivity Merry-Go-Round of Doom; endlessly cycling between burnout and procrastination. As the pace picked up in the Spring, I would work until I dropped: not eating, not resting, not exercising, and certainly not enjoying my life. Then, when the pace pulled back in the Summer, I found that I couldn't do anything beyond the bare minimum. I would set goals designed to get me ahead of the curve but just putzed around instead.

After three years of this, I reached a severe breaking point. One weekend in April of my third year as a consultant, my stress level reached such a fever pitch that I checked in to the emergency room, certain I was having a heart attack.

I wasn't.

In that moment, I realized: If I was going to have a life worth living, things were going to have to change. I needed a way to do my job with more ease during the busy times and remain motivated and engaged when the pressure came off.

I started with traditional time management tools, building expertise in systems like "Getting Things Done," Kanban, Pomodoro, and time blocking. I learned some very effective tactics, many of which I still use today. And yet... though I was doing a better job of cycling through to-dos at work, I was getting no closer to what mattered *to me*.

And while we are on the subject... what *did* matter to me?

Just to be clear, this experience is not uniquely mine. This is most of us. Whether we are running a business, building a practice, climbing the corporate ladder, or creating a family life that feel authentic and nurturing: the vast majority of us spend our lives on autopilot, doing what we've always done and getting the results we've always gotten.

Despite all of the work I had done to maximize my time, this piece just wasn't changing. This is when I realized that ordinary time management is severely limited because it is premised on three false assumptions:

1. You remember what you want.
2. It helps to do more.
3. You are making choices about how you spend your time from a neutral, objective place.

The Aligned Time Journal assumes that all three of these are false.

1. **To remember what you want, you need to keep it top of mind.** You probably *regularly* lose sight of what you want. There are moments of clarity, for sure: In a surge of enthusiasm you set a goal, make some plans... and then get swept up into the tangled mess of other people's expectations, habit, prior commitments, and duty. Weeks, and sometimes months go by and you make *no progress* on your goals. This is a phenomenon I call "goalnesia" because it feels entirely out of your control, like selective amnesia. When you wake back up

to the goal that you set, you are confused and frustrated, wondering "Why didn't I do anything? What's wrong with me?!" The Aligned Time Journal combats goalnesia directly by reminding you every quarter, every week and every single day about what you want. As you keep it top of mind, you can begin to make progress.

2. **You must do less.** The key to doing more of what matters is doing much, much less of the things that don't matter. Let's call those tasks that come from outside expectations, habit, and duty "the Rest of It." The Aligned Time Journal supports you as you build a habit of saying no, backing out, and resisting the pull of "the Rest of It," thereby creating space for what matters. With that space created, you can pursue the goals that matter to you with fewer distractions and more energy.

3. **You have to stop operating from fear.** Most people experience a lot of fear about time management and goal setting. Fear, for its part, makes people act erratically about their goals, causing feelings of frustration and shame. I know that someone is fighting through fear to accomplish their goals if they are exhibiting the symptoms of hurry, worry, or guilt.

   ☺ **Hurry.** Are you desperate to "get this goal over with" so you can finally relax and feel good about yourself?

   ☹ **Worry.** Are you obsessed with the question of whether you are "the kind of person" who can do what you want to do? What if you just don't have what it takes and everyone finds out that you're a total fraud?!?

   ☺ **Guilt.** Do you feel guilty about pursuing your goals, certain that you are leaving people behind or acting selfishly?

The Aligned Time Journal will change the way you approach goal setting by aligning your time to your goals and letting go of "the rest of it." Every quarter, week, and day you'll be reminded of your goals, supported to say "no," and encouraged to let go your fear.

When you adjust your life a little bit every day, you will transform your life without ever feeling overwhelmed. Before you know it, you'll be doing less, accomplishing more, and feeling a deep sense of integrity.

This is the purpose of the Aligned Time Journal.

QUICK START GUIDE

1 Set aside an hour to determine your three goals.

2 Once a week, set aside half an hour to reflect on last week and plan your upcoming week.

3 Every day, find a total of 20 minutes to check in on the previous day and plan how you'll spend your time that day. Some people do a 10 minute plan in the morning and a 10 minute reflection at night, while others prefer to do both in the morning. It's your choice!

4 Repeat!

LIFE IS A REFLECTION OF WHAT WE ALLOW OURSELVES TO SEE.

—Trudy Symeonakis Vesotsky

SET YOUR 90-DAY GOALS

EVERY 90 DAYS, YOU WILL check in on your vision and set new goals. This is the fun part! (Actually, it's all fun.)

Here's how to get the most from these exercises:

⏱ Carve Out Time

Schedule an hour of quiet and uninterrupted time. You'll use it to plan your goals for the next 90 days.

Note: I suggest taking a five-minute break between "The Good Life" and the "Next 90 Days," where you see the hand.

🔨 Be Decisive

There are a lot of decisions to make in the first few exercises. Do NOT stress about your choices! If you aren't careful, these exercises will take much longer than is ideal. Follow your intuition, be decisive, and know that whatever you choose will get you where you need to go.

☺ Be Realistic, but Not Right Away

Begin the vision work without ANY effort to be realistic. Plumb the depths of your desire and figure out what would delight you. What would get you out of bed? What would blow your mind? When you arrive at "The Next 90 Days" page, you will switch to a more concrete mindset. But until then, get (and stay) excited.

👁 Know That a Great Vision Is One That Inspires You To Greatness

This means that your best visions will feel a little scary, and maybe a little cocky, selfish, or unrealistic. Don't shut yourself down! Trust me, we'll find a way for you to pursue your desires without losing your core or violating your values.

Want more guidance on how to begin? Grab the Aligned Time Resource Pack at amandacrowell.com/aligned-time

WEB OF LIFE

LET'S START BY IDENTIFYING WHAT matters most to you in your life and business.

Step 1: Read through the three lists below.

Step 2: Make this list your own: You can add any categories you feel are missing, break my categories apart, or smush two of my categories together. This is just a place to start.

Step 3: Choose 12 areas to include in your web of life on the next page.

♥ Life

- Intimate relationships
- Friendship
- Family
- Personal or Family Finances
- Social life
- Career
- Hobbies
- Creativity
- Adventure
- Spirituality
- Physical space/home
- Personal development
-
-

🐾 Business Building

- Client creation/Sales
- Business Finances
- Events
- Networking/Outreach
- Content Creation
- Writing/Speaking
- Products/Courses
- Website
-
-

🧘 Self-Care

- Meditation
- Sleep/Downtime
- Time Alone
- Exercise
-
-

💡 Your Ideas

-
-

Creating Your Web of Life

1. **Choose twelve areas of your life that matter to you from the lists on the preceding page.** Write one per circle in the Web of Life on page 10.

2. **Mark how satisfied you are in each area of your life** by placing a dot on the line between the word "low" and the circle. The closer to the word "low," the less satisfied you are. Connect the dots with a line to see your web of satisfaction.

3. **Rank order these from 1-12 according to their priority to you.** In the smaller outer circles, give each area a rank order. Force yourself to choose between items that feel identical in their priority to you.

4. **Notice what you notice.** Are there areas of your life that are high priority and low satisfaction? These might be areas where you could make some progress in the next 90 days.

5. **Choose five areas of your life where you would like to make some progress.** This can involve optimizing an area that is already strong, building up an area where you'd like to be stronger, or working on an area that is a high priority with lower than desired satisfaction. Write them on page 10, one per area in the "Good Life: One Year From Now."

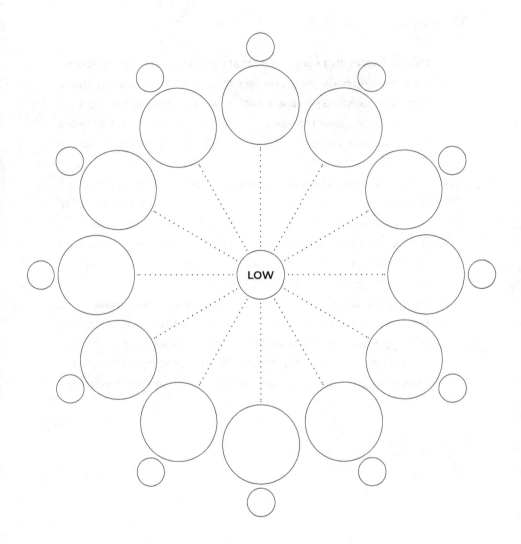

Choose five areas of your life in which you would like to make some progress. Write one per circle:

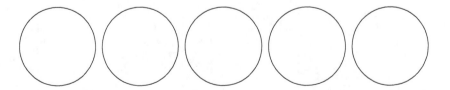

THE GOOD LIFE:
ONE YEAR FROM NOW

⚡ **Brainstorm Instructions:**

First, write the five areas you chose from your Web of Life in the five sections on the next page.

Then, identify some aspirations for each section:

📅 What do you want to be true in one year?

💓 What do you want your life to look like?

🕊 What do you hope will have happened?

🌱 To what do you aspire?

Think in term of concrete accomplishments and write them as if they are true.

For example: "One year from now..."

▸ I have nine clients
▸ I make $300,000
▸ I have finished the course I've been working on

⏱ **Take five minutes for each section and generate as many aspirations as you can.**

⭐ **Pro Tip:** Don't judge your brainstorm! Feel free to believe in the impossible and hope for the best. We'll be realistic when we're planning our goals, but when you are setting your vision, don't worry about "how" things will happen or "whether they're even possible." Also, don't worry if you "couldn't possibly do it all."

Right now, we are simply asking: **What do you want your life to look like in a year?**

Area 1: ....

Area 2: ....

Area 3: ....

Area 4: ....

Area 5: ....

Now, look over your brainstorm and **circle the three aspirations** that you are most excited to make progress on over the next 90 days. We will use these to create goals on the next page.

The Aligned Time Journal is built on the 3S Goal Structure: one goal that stretches you (Stretch), one that helps make the stretch possible (Support), and one that helps you feel grounded (Sanity).

An example:
I want to start speaking (Stretch), I would love to be more organized with my contracts and paperwork (Support), and I need to exercise at least twice a week (Sanity Goal).

On the next page you will be asked to choose which of your three aspirations feels like a stretch goal, which feels like a support goal, and which one feels like a sanity goal.

⭐ **Pro Tip:** It helps to identify your chosen **stretch** goal first!

✋ ON THE NEXT PAGE, WE ARE MOVING FROM BRAINSTORMING INTO CONCRETE GOALS WORK.

NOW WOULD BE A GREAT TIME TO TAKE A BREAK.

THE NEXT 90 DAYS

FILL IN THE FOLLOWING BLANKS with the three aspirations that you are most excited to make progress on over the next 90 days.

Then use the prompts to translate these aspirations into 90-day goals.

◎ Which goal? ○ Stretch   ○ Support   ○ Sanity

In one year, I aspire to:

Now, let's translate that one-year aspiration into a 90-day goal:

How can I get a little closer to this in the next 90 days?

Does accomplishing this in the next 90 days overwhelm me? If yes, how can I make it more doable?* (Once you feel good about your goal, copy it onto the relevant goal planning page.)

◎ Which goal? ○ Stretch   ○ Support   ○ Sanity

In one year, I aspire to:

Now, let's translate that one-year aspiration into a 90-day goal:

How can I get a little closer to this in the next 90 days?

Does accomplishing this in the next 90 days overwhelm me? If yes, how can I make it more doable?* (Once you feel good about your goal, copy it onto the relevant goal planning page.)

◎ **Which goal?**   O Stretch   O Support   O Sanity
In one year, I aspire to:

Now, let's translate that one-year aspiration into a 90-day goal:
How can I get a little closer to this in the next 90 days?

Does accomplishing this in the next 90 days overwhelm me? If yes, how can I make it more doable?* (Once you feel good about your goal, copy it onto the relevant goal planning page.)

*A smaller goal you can accomplish in 90 days **is always better** than a bigger goal that completely overwhelms you and causes you to stumble.

You can have everything you want,
but not all at the same time.

—Amanda Crowell

◎ MY STRETCH GOAL FOR THE NEXT 90 DAYS IS:

♥ Why does this goal matter to me?

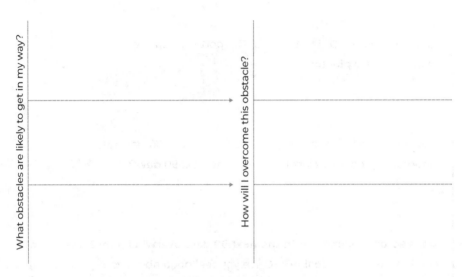

What obstacles are likely to get in my way?

How will I overcome this obstacle?

💧 What resources do I have to help me achieve this goal?
Who can I ask for help?

⚡ Brainstorm small steps that you can take right away. Whenever you get stuck, you can return to this list and begin again. Don't worry if you don't fill every line—as ideas occur to you over the next 90 days, you can add them to the list.

○ ....

○ ....

○ ....

○ ....

○ ....

○ ....

◎ **MY SUPPORT GOAL FOR THE NEXT 90 DAYS IS:**

♥ Why does this goal matter to me?

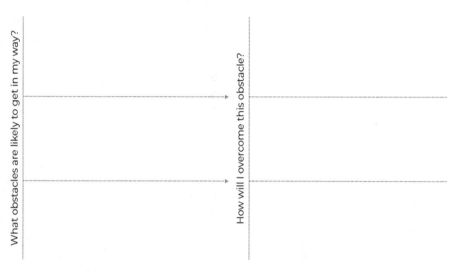

◌ What resources do I have to help me achieve this goal?
Who can I ask for help?

⚡ Brainstorm small steps that you can take right away. Whenever you get stuck, you can return to this list and begin again. Don't worry if you don't fill every line—as ideas occur to you over the next 90 days, you can add them to the list.

○ ....

○ ....

○ ....

○ ....

○ ....

○ ....

◎ MY SANITY GOAL FOR THE NEXT 90 DAYS IS:

♥ Why does this goal matter to me?

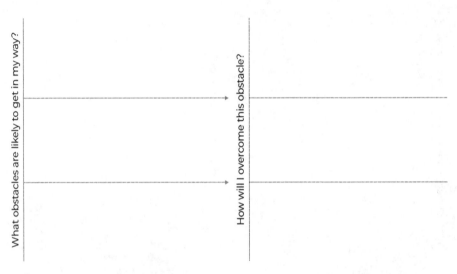

What obstacles are likely to get in my way?

How will I overcome this obstacle?

💧 What resources do I have to help me achieve this goal?
Who can I ask for help?

⚡ Brainstorm small steps that you can take right away. Whenever you get stuck, you can return to this list and begin again. Don't worry if you don't fill every line—as ideas occur to you over the next 90 days, you can add them to the list.

○ ....

○ ....

○ ....

○ ....

○ ....

○ ....

**WANT MORE GUIDANCE
ON HOW TO GET STARTED
AND STAY MOTIVATED?
GRAB THE ALIGNED TIME
RESOURCE PACK**

⌄

amanda.crowell.com/aligned-time

**NOTHING IS
PARTICULARLY HARD
IF YOU BREAK IT
INTO SMALL JOBS.**

—Henry Ford

REFLECT AND SET YOUR WEEKLY TASKS

EVERY WEEK, YOU'LL REVIEW THE previous week and plan the next.

Here's how to get the most from your weekly practice:

Make It a Habit

Schedule the time on your calendar to plan and reflect on your week. Give yourself about half an hour of quiet and uninterrupted time.

Be Balanced

As you get started, it's useful to choose one weekly task for each of your three goals. This will help you quickly learn what it takes to make progress on these goals.

Be Realistic

It's important that you balance your goals against your existing commitments. As you plan your week, make sure you consult your calendar and take on three tasks that can be realistically accomplished.

Keep It Short

Reviewing the previous week and planning the next should take between 20 and 30 minutes. Do not allow it to go much longer than that. It's important that you do not let the process overwhelm you.

Bounce Back

If you forget to plan one week, don't worry! It happens to us all. If you remember during the week, go ahead and plan for what's left. And if you forget for a whole week, don't try to catch up! Just start up with the week you are in and keep moving forward.

○ I reviewed my 90-day goals

➲ HOW CAN I GET A LITTLE CLOSER TO MY GOALS THIS WEEK?

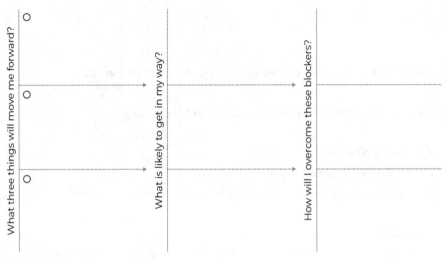

⊘ What will I say NO to this week?

🕴 How can I keep my life in balance this week?

📅 WEEKLY REFLECTION

🕘 What are my three favorite memories from this week?

1   2   3

✔ Did I do what I said I would do this week?
What can I learn from this?

🏃 How am I progressing against my 90-day goals?

○ I reviewed my 90-day goals

➔ HOW CAN I GET A LITTLE CLOSER TO MY GOALS THIS WEEK?

What three things will move me forward?

○

○

○

What is likely to get in my way?

How will I overcome these blockers?

🚫 What will I say NO to this week?

🧍 How can I keep my life in balance this week?

📅 WEEKLY REFLECTION

🕑 What are my three favorite memories from this week?

1

2

3

✅ Did I do what I said I would do this week?
What can I learn from this?

🏃 How am I progressing against my 90-day goals?

○ I reviewed my 90-day goals   //ALIGNING WEEK 3 .... TO ....

DATE RANGE

➡ HOW CAN I GET A LITTLE CLOSER TO MY GOALS THIS WEEK?

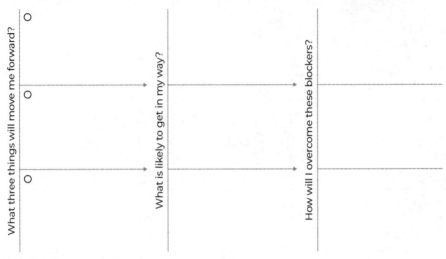

What three things will move me forward?

What is likely to get in my way?

How will I overcome these blockers?

⊘ What will I say NO to this week?

🜊 How can I keep my life in balance this week?

📅 WEEKLY REFLECTION

🕘 What are my three favorite memories from this week?

1 | 2 | 3

✔ Did I do what I said I would do this week?
What can I learn from this?

🏃 How am I progressing against my 90-day goals?

○ I reviewed my 90-day goals   //ALIGNING WEEK 4 .... TO ....

DATE RANGE

➔ HOW CAN I GET A LITTLE CLOSER TO MY GOALS THIS WEEK?

What three things will move me forward?

○

○

○

What is likely to get in my way?

How will I overcome these blockers?

🚫 What will I say NO to this week?

🧍 How can I keep my life in balance this week?

📅 WEEKLY REFLECTION

🕐 What are my three favorite memories from this week?

1

2

3

✅ Did I do what I said I would do this week?
What can I learn from this?

🏃 How am I progressing against my 90-day goals?

○ I reviewed my 90-day goals   //ALIGNING WEEK 5 .... TO ....

DATE RANGE

➔ **HOW CAN I GET A LITTLE CLOSER TO MY GOALS THIS WEEK?**

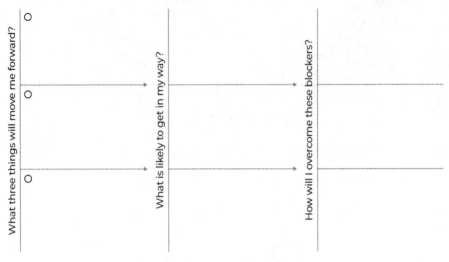

🚫 What will I say NO to this week?

🕴 How can I keep my life in balance this week?

📅 **WEEKLY REFLECTION**

🕐 What are my three favorite memories from this week?

1 | 2 | 3

✅ Did I do what I said I would do this week?
What can I learn from this?

🏃 How am I progressing against my 90-day goals?

○ I reviewed my 90-day goals

➲ HOW CAN I GET A LITTLE CLOSER TO MY GOALS THIS WEEK?

What three things will move me forward?

○

○

○

What is likely to get in my way?

How will I overcome these blockers?

🚫 What will I say NO to this week?

🧍 How can I keep my life in balance this week?

📅 WEEKLY REFLECTION

🕐 What are my three favorite memories from this week?

1

2

3

✅ Did I do what I said I would do this week?
What can I learn from this?

🏃 How am I progressing against my 90-day goals?

○ I reviewed my 90-day goals

➲ HOW CAN I GET A LITTLE CLOSER TO MY GOALS THIS WEEK?

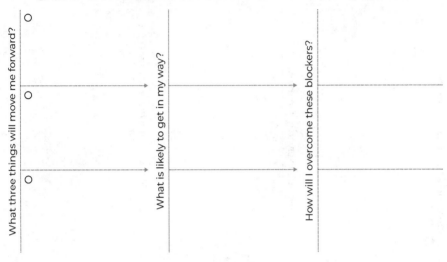

What three things will move me forward?

○

○

○

What is likely to get in my way?

How will I overcome these blockers?

⊘ What will I say NO to this week?

🧍 How can I keep my life in balance this week?

📅 WEEKLY REFLECTION

🕘 What are my three favorite memories from this week?

1 |

2 |

3 |

✔ Did I do what I said I would do this week?
What can I learn from this?

🏃 How am I progressing against my 90-day goals?

○ I reviewed my 90-day goals

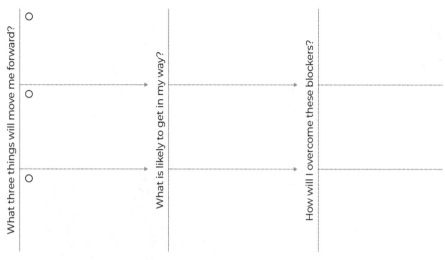

● HOW CAN I GET A LITTLE CLOSER TO MY GOALS THIS WEEK?

What three things will move me forward?

What is likely to get in my way?

How will I overcome these blockers?

🚫 What will I say NO to this week?

🧍 How can I keep my life in balance this week?

📅 WEEKLY REFLECTION

🕐 What are my three favorite memories from this week?

1

2

3

✔ Did I do what I said I would do this week?
What can I learn from this?

🏃 How am I progressing against my 90-day goals?

○ I reviewed my 90-day goals

➲ HOW CAN I GET A LITTLE CLOSER TO MY GOALS THIS WEEK?

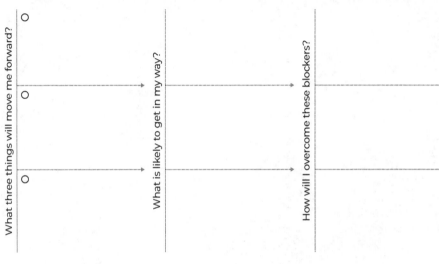

⃠ What will I say NO to this week?

👤 How can I keep my life in balance this week?

📅 WEEKLY REFLECTION

🕐 What are my three favorite memories from this week?

1   2   3

✅ Did I do what I said I would do this week?
What can I learn from this?

🏃 How am I progressing against my 90-day goals?

○ I reviewed my 90-day goals

➲ HOW CAN I GET A LITTLE CLOSER TO MY GOALS THIS WEEK?

What three things will move me forward?

○

○

○

What is likely to get in my way?

How will I overcome these blockers?

⊘ What will I say NO to this week?

☗ How can I keep my life in balance this week?

📅 WEEKLY REFLECTION

⟲ What are my three favorite memories from this week?

1

2

3

✔ Did I do what I said I would do this week?
What can I learn from this?

🏃 How am I progressing against my 90-day goals?

○ I reviewed my 90-day goals

➜ HOW CAN I GET A LITTLE CLOSER TO MY GOALS THIS WEEK?

What three things will move me forward?

○

○

○

What is likely to get in my way?

How will I overcome these blockers?

⊘ What will I say NO to this week?

🧍 How can I keep my life in balance this week?

🗓 WEEKLY REFLECTION

🕒 What are my three favorite memories from this week?

1

2

3

✅ Did I do what I said I would do this week?
What can I learn from this?

🏃 How am I progressing against my 90-day goals?

IT'S TIME
TO
REORDER!

⌄

amanda.crowell.com/aligned-time

○ I reviewed my 90-day goals

➦ HOW CAN I GET A LITTLE CLOSER TO MY GOALS THIS WEEK?

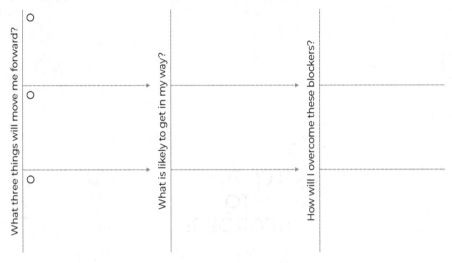

What three things will move me forward?

○

○

○

What is likely to get in my way?

How will I overcome these blockers?

🚫 What will I say NO to this week?

🧍 How can I keep my life in balance this week?

📅 WEEKLY REFLECTION

🕒 What are my three favorite memories from this week?

1 |

2 |

3 |

✅ Did I do what I said I would do this week?
What can I learn from this?

🏃 How am I progressing against my 90-day goals?

○ I reviewed my 90-day goals

➡ HOW CAN I GET A LITTLE CLOSER TO MY GOALS THIS WEEK?

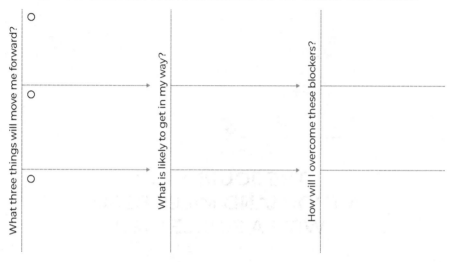

What three things will move me forward?

○

○

○

What is likely to get in my way?

How will I overcome these blockers?

🚫 What will I say NO to this week?

🧍 How can I keep my life in balance this week?

📅 WEEKLY REFLECTION

🔄 What are my three favorite memories from this week?

1

2

3

✅ Did I do what I said I would do this week?
What can I learn from this?

🏃 How am I progressing against my 90-day goals?

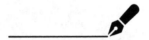

THE JOURNEY OF
A THOUSAND MILES BEGINS
WITH A SINGLE STEP.

—Lao Tzu

REFLECT AND SET YOUR DAILY TO-DOS

THIS IS WHERE YOU ALIGN your time to your goals every day. It's the heart of The Aligned Time Journal experience.

Here's how to get the most from your daily practice.

⚓ **Create a *Convenient* Routine**

It's best to complete this activity at the same time and place each day. Try to anchor it into an already existing habit, such as quiet time while drinking your coffee, or after you work out but before your shower.

📅 **Be Realistic**

It's important that you balance your goals against your existing commitments. As you plan your day, make sure you've looked at your calendar and take on three tasks that can *realistically* be accomplished.

📓 **Keep the Aligned Time Journal Visible**

It helps to leave your journal out and about or carry it with you in your bag. This will keep it top of mind as you go about your day

🏀 **Bounce Back**

If you happen to fall out of the habit for a few days, don't worry! It happens to us all. Don't try to catch up! Just start back up today and keep moving forward.

➘ **Keep It short**

The entire daily practice should take between 10 and 15 minutes. Keep it contained, as it's important that you do not let the process overwhelm you.

⠿ **When You Stumble, Go Smaller**

If you notice a pattern of something not getting done across multiple days, break it into a smaller task and give yourself a win.

○ I reviewed my weekly tasks

♥ I am grateful for:

Because:

☀ HOW CAN I GET A LITTLE CLOSER TO MY GOALS TODAY?

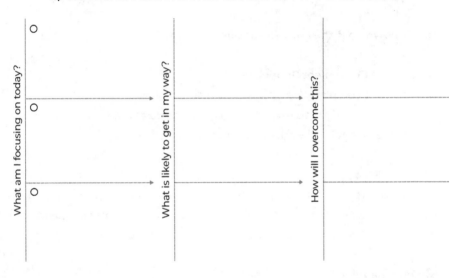

⊘ What will I say NO to today?

☾ DAILY REFLECTION

⟳ What's my favorite memory from today?

✔ Did I do what I said I would do?

What can I learn from this?

○ I reviewed my weekly tasks

♥ I am grateful for:

Because:

☀ **HOW CAN I GET A LITTLE CLOSER TO MY GOALS TODAY?**

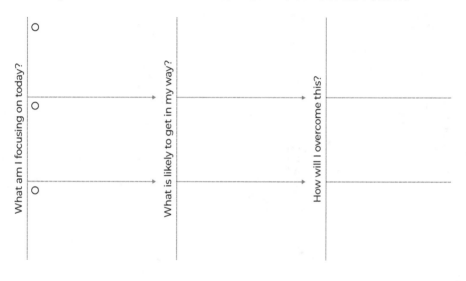

⊘ What will I say NO to today?

☾ **DAILY REFLECTION**

⟲ What's my favorite memory from today?

✔ Did I do what I said I would do?

What can I learn from this?

○ I reviewed my weekly tasks

♥ I am grateful for:
Because:

☀ **HOW CAN I GET A LITTLE CLOSER TO MY GOALS TODAY?**

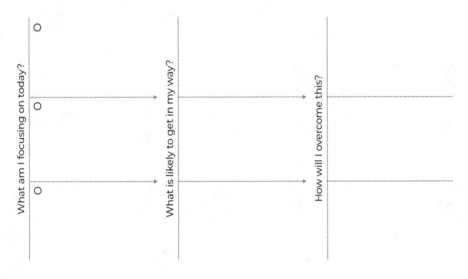

⊘ What will I say NO to today?

☾ **DAILY REFLECTION**

↺ What's my favorite memory from today?

✔ Did I do what I said I would do?
What can I learn from this?

○ I reviewed my weekly tasks

♥ I am grateful for:

Because:

☀ HOW CAN I GET A LITTLE CLOSER TO MY GOALS TODAY?

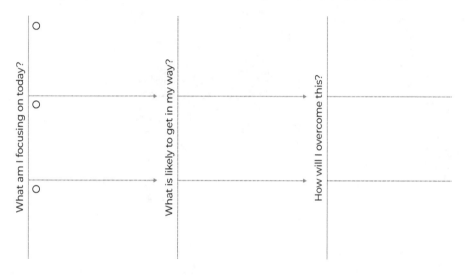

🚫 What will I say NO to today?

☾ DAILY REFLECTION

🕘 What's my favorite memory from today?

✅ Did I do what I said I would do?

What can I learn from this?

○ I reviewed my weekly tasks   //**ALIGNING TODAY** ..../.........../.............

♥ I am grateful for:

Because:

☀ HOW CAN I GET A LITTLE CLOSER TO MY GOALS TODAY?

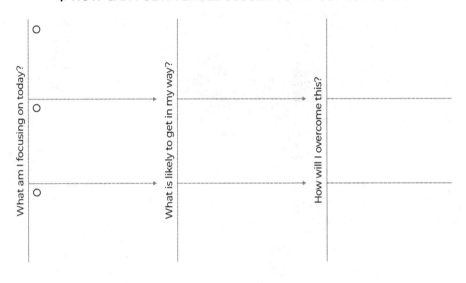

⊘ What will I say NO to today?

☾ DAILY REFLECTION

⟳ What's my favorite memory from today?

✔ Did I do what I said I would do?

What can I learn from this?

○ I reviewed my weekly tasks

♥ I am grateful for:

Because:

☀ HOW CAN I GET A LITTLE CLOSER TO MY GOALS TODAY?

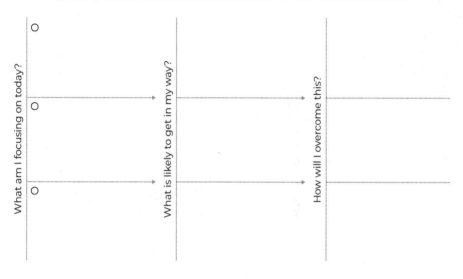

What am I focusing on today?

What is likely to get in my way?

How will I overcome this?

🚫 What will I say NO to today?

☾ DAILY REFLECTION

🔃 What's my favorite memory from today?

✅ Did I do what I said I would do?

What can I learn from this?

○ I reviewed my weekly tasks

♥ I am grateful for:

Because:

☀ HOW CAN I GET A LITTLE CLOSER TO MY GOALS TODAY?

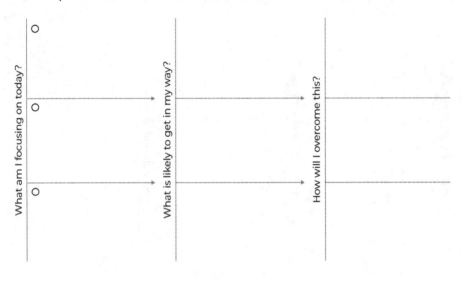

⊘ What will I say NO to today?

☾ DAILY REFLECTION

↺ What's my favorite memory from today?

✔ Did I do what I said I would do?

What can I learn from this?

○ I reviewed my weekly tasks

♥ I am grateful for:

Because:

☼ HOW CAN I GET A LITTLE CLOSER TO MY GOALS TODAY?

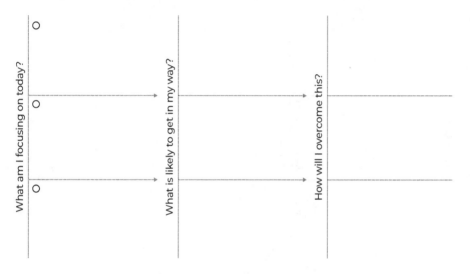

○ What will I say NO to today?

☾ DAILY REFLECTION

↻ What's my favorite memory from today?

✔ Did I do what I said I would do?

What can I learn from this?

○ I reviewed my weekly tasks   //ALIGNING TODAY ..../........./..............

♥ I am grateful for:

Because:

☀ HOW CAN I GET A LITTLE CLOSER TO MY GOALS TODAY?

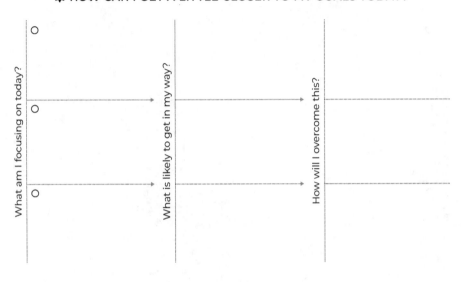

⊘ What will I say NO to today?

☾ DAILY REFLECTION

⟲ What's my favorite memory from today?

✔ Did I do what I said I would do?

What can I learn from this?

○ I reviewed my weekly tasks

♥ I am grateful for:

Because:

☀ HOW CAN I GET A LITTLE CLOSER TO MY GOALS TODAY?

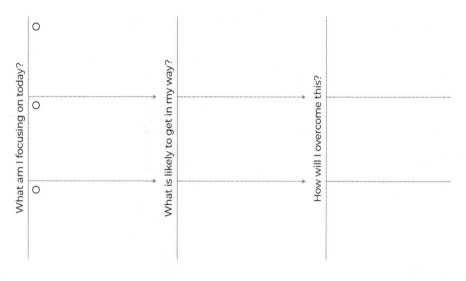

⊘ What will I say NO to today?

☾ DAILY REFLECTION

⟲ What's my favorite memory from today?

✔ Did I do what I said I would do?

What can I learn from this?

○ I reviewed my weekly tasks

♥ I am grateful for:

Because:

☀ HOW CAN I GET A LITTLE CLOSER TO MY GOALS TODAY?

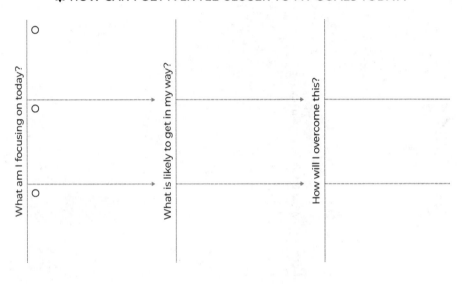

⊘ What will I say NO to today?

☾ DAILY REFLECTION

⟲ What's my favorite memory from today?

✔ Did I do what I said I would do?

What can I learn from this?

○ I reviewed my weekly tasks　　　　//**ALIGNING TODAY** ..../........../..........

♥ I am grateful for:

Because:

☀ HOW CAN I GET A LITTLE CLOSER TO MY GOALS TODAY?

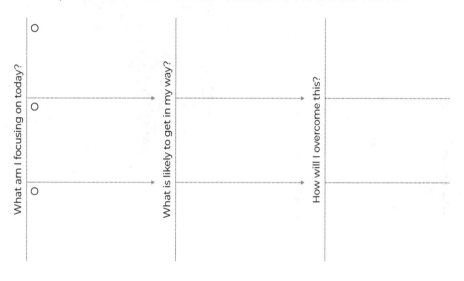

🚫 What will I say NO to today?

☾ DAILY REFLECTION

🕲 What's my favorite memory from today?

✔ Did I do what I said I would do?

What can I learn from this?

○ I reviewed my weekly tasks

♥ I am grateful for:

Because:

☀ HOW CAN I GET A LITTLE CLOSER TO MY GOALS TODAY?

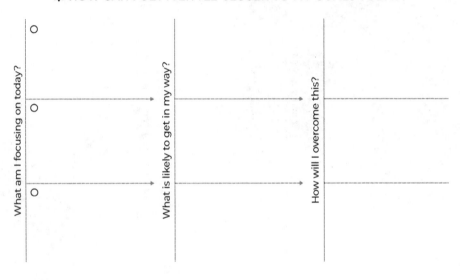

What am I focusing on today?

What is likely to get in my way?

How will I overcome this?

⊘ What will I say NO to today?

☾ DAILY REFLECTION

⟲ What's my favorite memory from today?

✔ Did I do what I said I would do?

What can I learn from this?

○ I reviewed my weekly tasks   **//ALIGNING TODAY** ..../........./..........

♥ I am grateful for:
Because:

☀ HOW CAN I GET A LITTLE CLOSER TO MY GOALS TODAY?

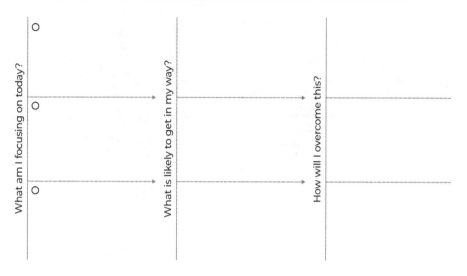

⊘ What will I say NO to today?

☾ DAILY REFLECTION

↻ What's my favorite memory from today?

✔ Did I do what I said I would do?
What can I learn from this?

○ I reviewed my weekly tasks   **//ALIGNING TODAY** ..../.........../.............

♥ I am grateful for:

Because:

☀ HOW CAN I GET A LITTLE CLOSER TO MY GOALS TODAY?

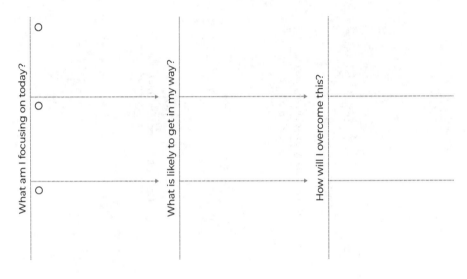

🚫 What will I say NO to today?

☾ DAILY REFLECTION

🕘 What's my favorite memory from today?

✔ Did I do what I said I would do?

What can I learn from this?

○ I reviewed my weekly tasks

♥ I am grateful for:
Because:

☀ HOW CAN I GET A LITTLE CLOSER TO MY GOALS TODAY?

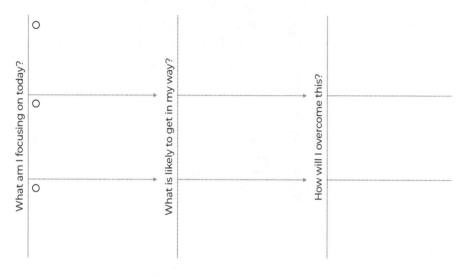

⦸ What will I say NO to today?

☾ DAILY REFLECTION

↺ What's my favorite memory from today?

✔ Did I do what I said I would do?
What can I learn from this?

○ I reviewed my weekly tasks

♥ I am grateful for:

Because:

☀ HOW CAN I GET A LITTLE CLOSER TO MY GOALS TODAY?

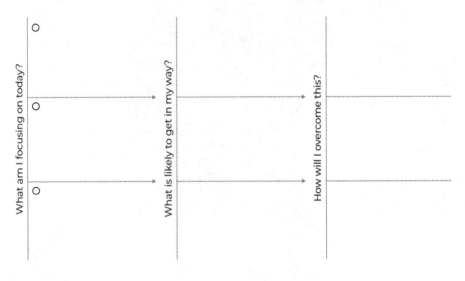

⊘ What will I say NO to today?

☾ DAILY REFLECTION

⟲ What's my favorite memory from today?

✔ Did I do what I said I would do?

What can I learn from this?

○ I reviewed my weekly tasks   **//ALIGNING TODAY** ..../............/............

♥ I am grateful for:

Because:

☼ HOW CAN I GET A LITTLE CLOSER TO MY GOALS TODAY?

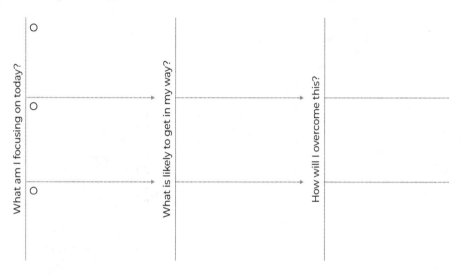

⊘ What will I say NO to today?

☾ DAILY REFLECTION

⟲ What's my favorite memory from today?

✔ Did I do what I said I would do?

What can I learn from this?

○ I reviewed my weekly tasks

♥ I am grateful for:

Because:

☀ HOW CAN I GET A LITTLE CLOSER TO MY GOALS TODAY?

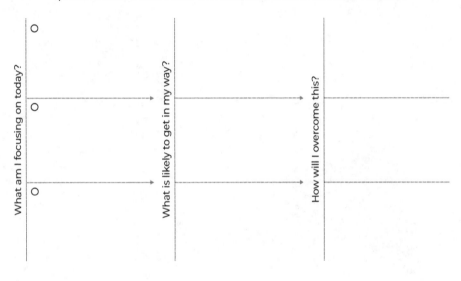

○ What will I say NO to today?

☾ DAILY REFLECTION

↺ What's my favorite memory from today?

✔ Did I do what I said I would do?

What can I learn from this?

○ I reviewed my weekly tasks

♥ I am grateful for:

Because:

☀ HOW CAN I GET A LITTLE CLOSER TO MY GOALS TODAY?

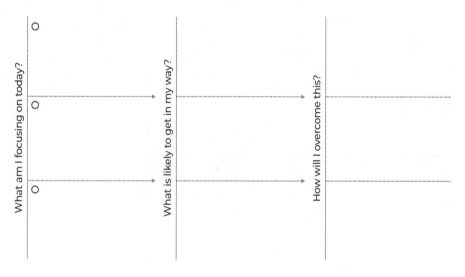

What am I focusing on today?

What is likely to get in my way?

How will I overcome this?

⊘ What will I say NO to today?

☾ DAILY REFLECTION

↺ What's my favorite memory from today?

✔ Did I do what I said I would do?

What can I learn from this?

○ I reviewed my weekly tasks　　　**//ALIGNING TODAY** ..../.........../.............

♥ I am grateful for:

Because:

☀ HOW CAN I GET A LITTLE CLOSER TO MY GOALS TODAY?

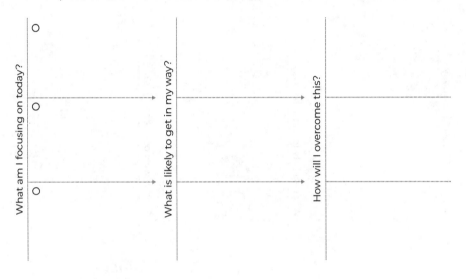

⊘ What will I say NO to today?

☾ DAILY REFLECTION

🕗 What's my favorite memory from today?

✔ Did I do what I said I would do?

What can I learn from this?

○ I reviewed my weekly tasks

♥ I am grateful for:

Because:

☀ HOW CAN I GET A LITTLE CLOSER TO MY GOALS TODAY?

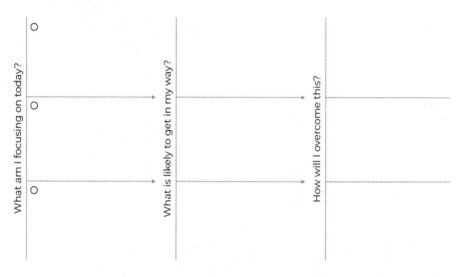

○ What will I say NO to today?

☾ DAILY REFLECTION

↺ What's my favorite memory from today?

✔ Did I do what I said I would do?

What can I learn from this?

○ I reviewed my weekly tasks   **//ALIGNING TODAY** ..../.........../............

♥ I am grateful for:

Because:

☀ HOW CAN I GET A LITTLE CLOSER TO MY GOALS TODAY?

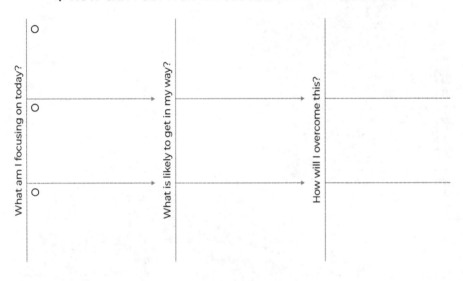

What am I focusing on today?

What is likely to get in my way?

How will I overcome this?

🚫 What will I say NO to today?

☾ DAILY REFLECTION

⟳ What's my favorite memory from today?

✔ Did I do what I said I would do?

What can I learn from this?

○ I reviewed my weekly tasks

♥ I am grateful for:

Because:

☀ HOW CAN I GET A LITTLE CLOSER TO MY GOALS TODAY?

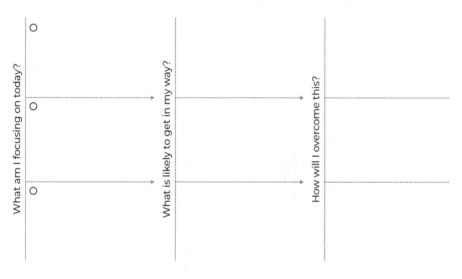

What am I focusing on today?

○

○

○

What is likely to get in my way?

How will I overcome this?

⊘ What will I say NO to today?

☾ DAILY REFLECTION

↺ What's my favorite memory from today?

✔ Did I do what I said I would do?

What can I learn from this?

○ I reviewed my weekly tasks

♥ I am grateful for:

Because:

☀ HOW CAN I GET A LITTLE CLOSER TO MY GOALS TODAY?

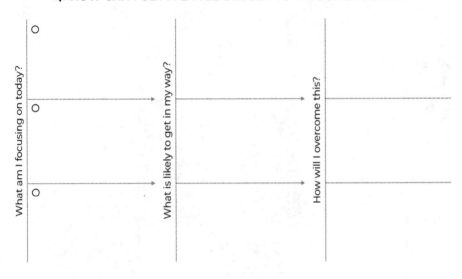

⊘ What will I say NO to today?

☾ DAILY REFLECTION

⟲ What's my favorite memory from today?

✔ Did I do what I said I would do?

What can I learn from this?

○ I reviewed my weekly tasks

♥ I am grateful for:

Because:

☼ HOW CAN I GET A LITTLE CLOSER TO MY GOALS TODAY?

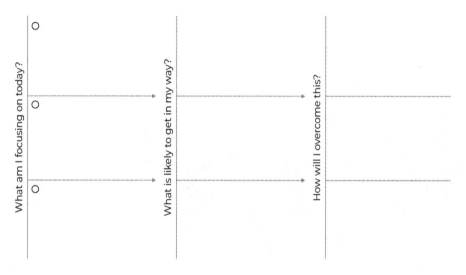

⊘ What will I say NO to today?

☾ DAILY REFLECTION

↻ What's my favorite memory from today?

✔ Did I do what I said I would do?

What can I learn from this?

○ I reviewed my weekly tasks

♥ I am grateful for:

Because:

☀ HOW CAN I GET A LITTLE CLOSER TO MY GOALS TODAY?

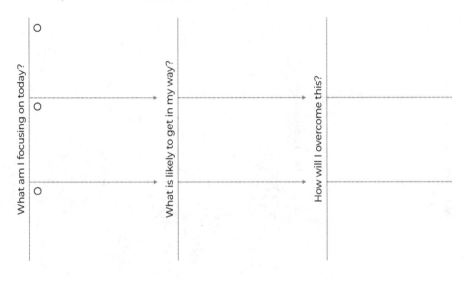

⊘ What will I say NO to today?

☾ DAILY REFLECTION

⟳ What's my favorite memory from today?

✔ Did I do what I said I would do?

What can I learn from this?

○ I reviewed my weekly tasks

♥ I am grateful for:

Because:

☀ HOW CAN I GET A LITTLE CLOSER TO MY GOALS TODAY?

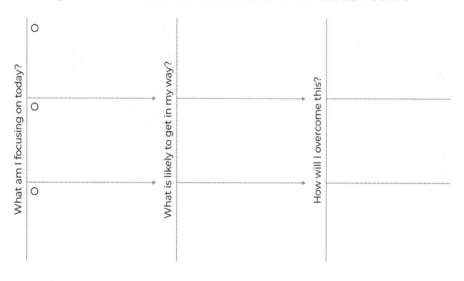

⊘ What will I say NO to today?

☾ DAILY REFLECTION

⟳ What's my favorite memory from today?

✔ Did I do what I said I would do?

What can I learn from this?

○ I reviewed my weekly tasks   **//ALIGNING TODAY** ..../.........../..............

♥ I am grateful for:

Because:

☼ HOW CAN I GET A LITTLE CLOSER TO MY GOALS TODAY?

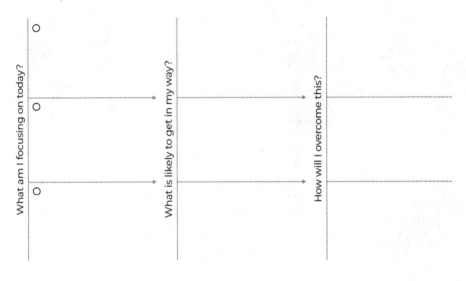

⊘ What will I say NO to today?

- -

☾ DAILY REFLECTION

⟳ What's my favorite memory from today?

✔ Did I do what I said I would do?

What can I learn from this?

○ I reviewed my weekly tasks

♥ I am grateful for:
Because:

☀ HOW CAN I GET A LITTLE CLOSER TO MY GOALS TODAY?

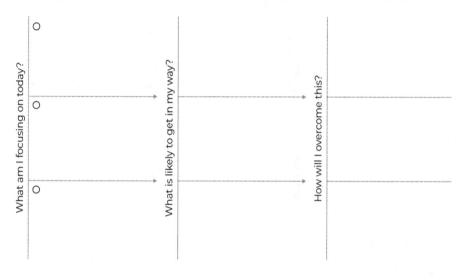

🚫 What will I say NO to today?

☾ DAILY REFLECTION

🕘 What's my favorite memory from today?

✔ Did I do what I said I would do?
What can I learn from this?

○ I reviewed my weekly tasks

♥ I am grateful for:
Because:

☀ HOW CAN I GET A LITTLE CLOSER TO MY GOALS TODAY?

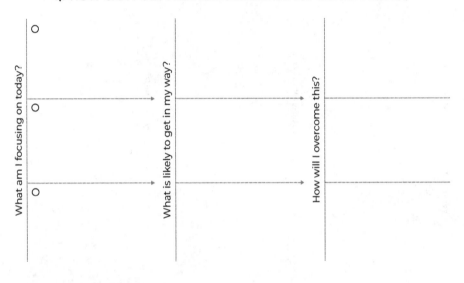

ⓢ What will I say NO to today?

☾ DAILY REFLECTION

↺ What's my favorite memory from today?

✔ Did I do what I said I would do?
What can I learn from this?

○ I reviewed my weekly tasks

♥ I am grateful for:
Because:

☼ HOW CAN I GET A LITTLE CLOSER TO MY GOALS TODAY?

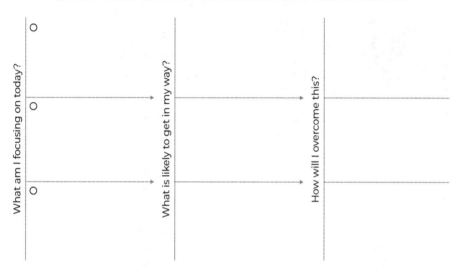

⊘ What will I say NO to today?

☾ DAILY REFLECTION

↺ What's my favorite memory from today?

✔ Did I do what I said I would do?
What can I learn from this?

○ I reviewed my weekly tasks

♥ I am grateful for:

Because:

☀ HOW CAN I GET A LITTLE CLOSER TO MY GOALS TODAY?

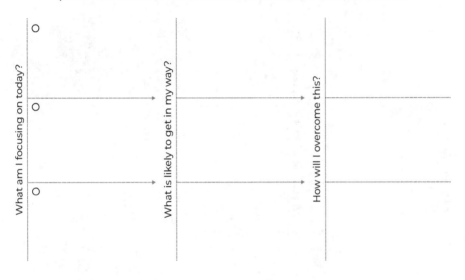

⊘ What will I say NO to today?

☾ DAILY REFLECTION

↺ What's my favorite memory from today?

✔ Did I do what I said I would do?

What can I learn from this?

○ I reviewed my weekly tasks

♥ I am grateful for:

Because:

☀ HOW CAN I GET A LITTLE CLOSER TO MY GOALS TODAY?

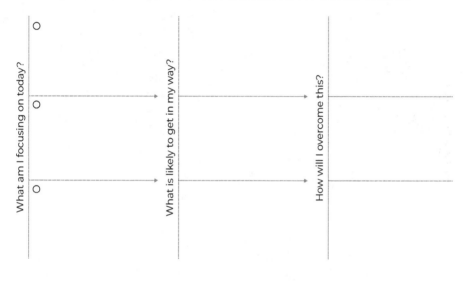

○ What will I say NO to today?

☾ DAILY REFLECTION

⟳ What's my favorite memory from today?

✔ Did I do what I said I would do?

What can I learn from this?

◯ I reviewed my weekly tasks

♥ I am grateful for:

Because:

☀ **HOW CAN I GET A LITTLE CLOSER TO MY GOALS TODAY?**

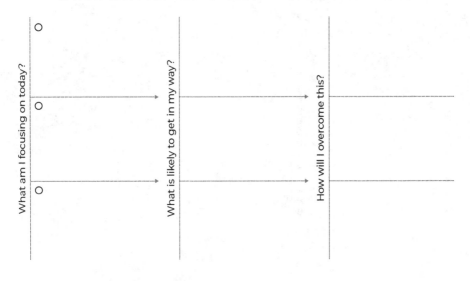

🚫 What will I say NO to today?

🌙 **DAILY REFLECTION**

⟳ What's my favorite memory from today?

✔ Did I do what I said I would do?

What can I learn from this?

○ I reviewed my weekly tasks   ///ALIGNING TODAY ..../......../........

♥ I am grateful for:
Because:

☼ HOW CAN I GET A LITTLE CLOSER TO MY GOALS TODAY?

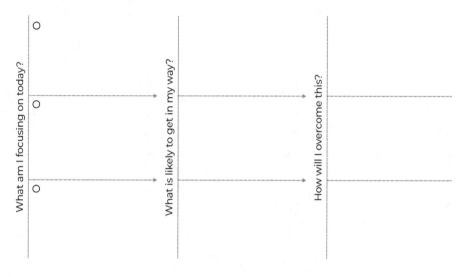

○ What will I say NO to today?

☾ DAILY REFLECTION

↻ What's my favorite memory from today?

✔ Did I do what I said I would do?
What can I learn from this?

○ I reviewed my weekly tasks

♥ I am grateful for:

Because:

☀ HOW CAN I GET A LITTLE CLOSER TO MY GOALS TODAY?

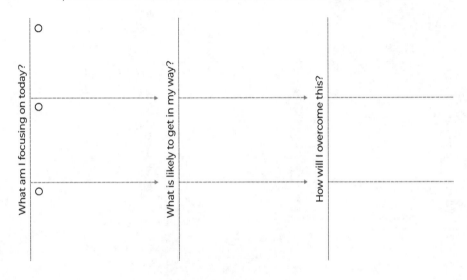

⊘ What will I say NO to today?

☾ DAILY REFLECTION

↺ What's my favorite memory from today?

✓ Did I do what I said I would do?

What can I learn from this?

○ I reviewed my weekly tasks   **//ALIGNING TODAY** ..../........../..........

♥ I am grateful for:

Because:

☀ HOW CAN I GET A LITTLE CLOSER TO MY GOALS TODAY?

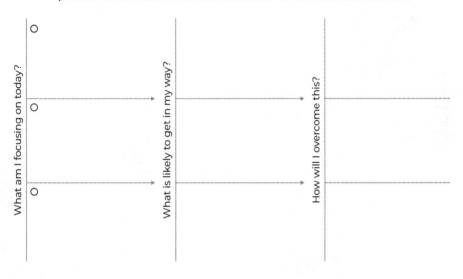

⊘ What will I say NO to today?

☾ DAILY REFLECTION

↺ What's my favorite memory from today?

✔ Did I do what I said I would do?

What can I learn from this?

○ I reviewed my weekly tasks   **//ALIGNING TODAY** ....../....../......

♥ I am grateful for:
Because:

☀ HOW CAN I GET A LITTLE CLOSER TO MY GOALS TODAY?

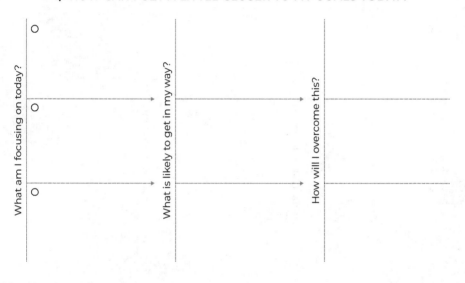

⊘ What will I say NO to today?

☾ DAILY REFLECTION

↺ What's my favorite memory from today?

✔ Did I do what I said I would do?
What can I learn from this?

○ I reviewed my weekly tasks

♥ I am grateful for:

Because:

☀ HOW CAN I GET A LITTLE CLOSER TO MY GOALS TODAY?

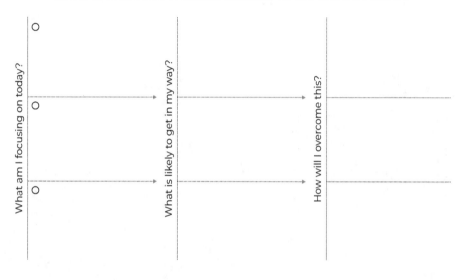

🚫 What will I say NO to today?

☾ DAILY REFLECTION

🕙 What's my favorite memory from today?

✔ Did I do what I said I would do?

What can I learn from this?

○ I reviewed my weekly tasks

♥ I am grateful for:

Because:

☀ HOW CAN I GET A LITTLE CLOSER TO MY GOALS TODAY?

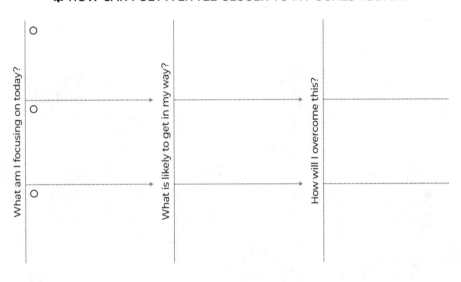

⊘ What will I say NO to today?

☾ DAILY REFLECTION

⟲ What's my favorite memory from today?

✔ Did I do what I said I would do?

What can I learn from this?

○ I reviewed my weekly tasks   **//ALIGNING TODAY** .... / .... / ....

♥ I am grateful for:

Because:

☀ HOW CAN I GET A LITTLE CLOSER TO MY GOALS TODAY?

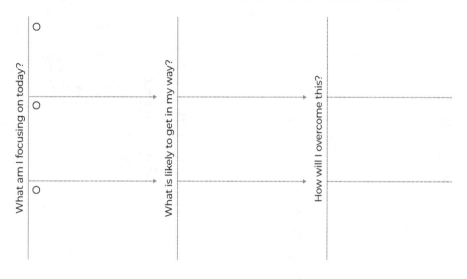

○ What will I say NO to today?

☾ DAILY REFLECTION

↺ What's my favorite memory from today?

✔ Did I do what I said I would do?

What can I learn from this?

○ I reviewed my weekly tasks

♥ I am grateful for:

Because:

☀ HOW CAN I GET A LITTLE CLOSER TO MY GOALS TODAY?

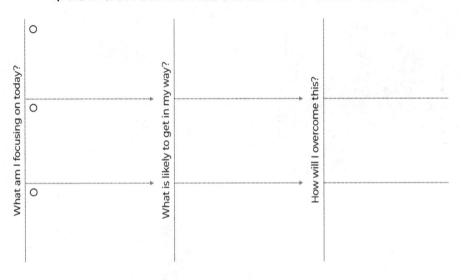

🚫 What will I say NO to today?

☾ DAILY REFLECTION

🕓 What's my favorite memory from today?

✓ Did I do what I said I would do?

What can I learn from this?

○ I reviewed my weekly tasks

♥ I am grateful for:

Because:

☀ HOW CAN I GET A LITTLE CLOSER TO MY GOALS TODAY?

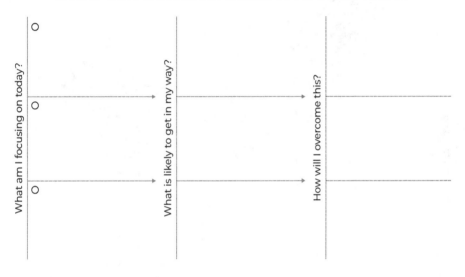

○ What will I say NO to today?

☾ DAILY REFLECTION

🕘 What's my favorite memory from today?

✔ Did I do what I said I would do?

What can I learn from this?

○ I reviewed my weekly tasks

♥ I am grateful for:

Because:

☀ HOW CAN I GET A LITTLE CLOSER TO MY GOALS TODAY?

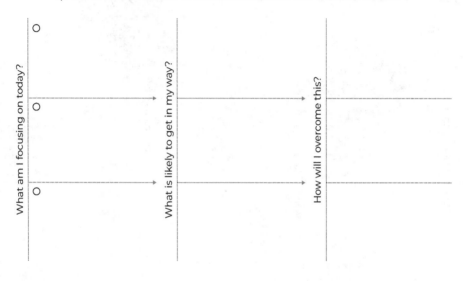

🚫 What will I say NO to today?

☾ DAILY REFLECTION

🕗 What's my favorite memory from today?

✔ Did I do what I said I would do?

What can I learn from this?

○ I reviewed my weekly tasks

♥ I am grateful for:
Because:

☀ HOW CAN I GET A LITTLE CLOSER TO MY GOALS TODAY?

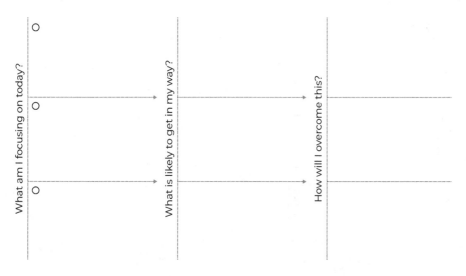

⃠ What will I say NO to today?

☾ DAILY REFLECTION

⟳ What's my favorite memory from today?

✔ Did I do what I said I would do?
What can I learn from this?

○ I reviewed my weekly tasks

♥ I am grateful for:

Because:

☀ HOW CAN I GET A LITTLE CLOSER TO MY GOALS TODAY?

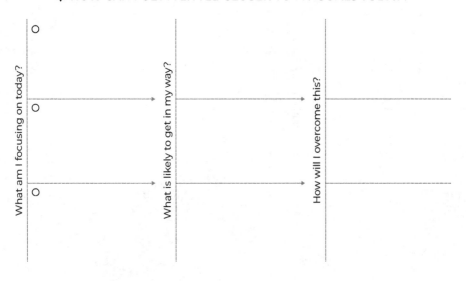

⊘ What will I say NO to today?

☾ DAILY REFLECTION

⟲ What's my favorite memory from today?

✔ Did I do what I said I would do?

What can I learn from this?

○ I reviewed my weekly tasks

♥ I am grateful for:

Because:

☀ HOW CAN I GET A LITTLE CLOSER TO MY GOALS TODAY?

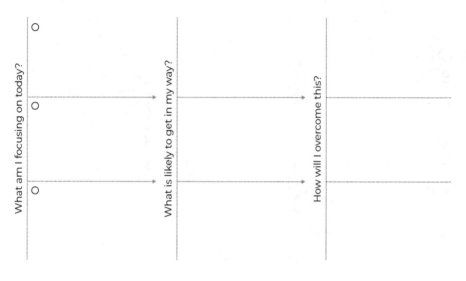

⊘ What will I say NO to today?

☾ DAILY REFLECTION

⟲ What's my favorite memory from today?

✔ Did I do what I said I would do?

What can I learn from this?

○ I reviewed my weekly tasks

♥ I am grateful for:

Because:

☀ HOW CAN I GET A LITTLE CLOSER TO MY GOALS TODAY?

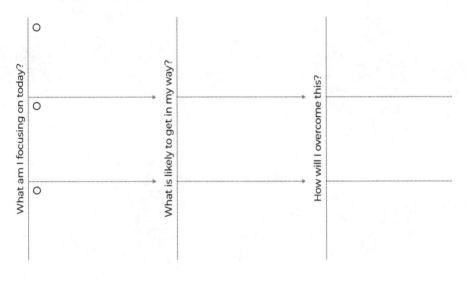

○ What will I say NO to today?

☾ DAILY REFLECTION

↻ What's my favorite memory from today?

✔ Did I do what I said I would do?

What can I learn from this?

○ I reviewed my weekly tasks   //**ALIGNING TODAY** ..../.........../..........

♥ I am grateful for:

Because:

☀ HOW CAN I GET A LITTLE CLOSER TO MY GOALS TODAY?

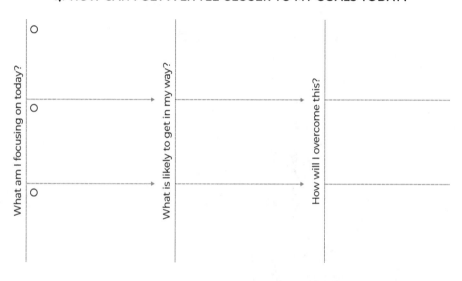

⊘ What will I say NO to today?

....

☾ DAILY REFLECTION

↻ What's my favorite memory from today?

✔ Did I do what I said I would do?

What can I learn from this?

○ I reviewed my weekly tasks

♥ I am grateful for:

Because:

☀ HOW CAN I GET A LITTLE CLOSER TO MY GOALS TODAY?

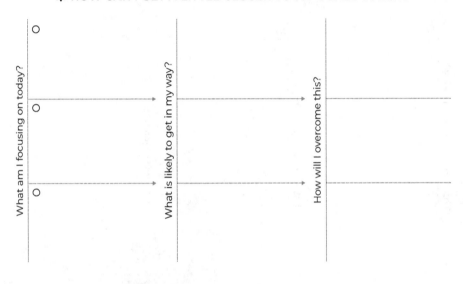

⃠ What will I say NO to today?

☾ DAILY REFLECTION

↺ What's my favorite memory from today?

✔ Did I do what I said I would do?

What can I learn from this?

○ I reviewed my weekly tasks

♥ I am grateful for:

Because:

☀ HOW CAN I GET A LITTLE CLOSER TO MY GOALS TODAY?

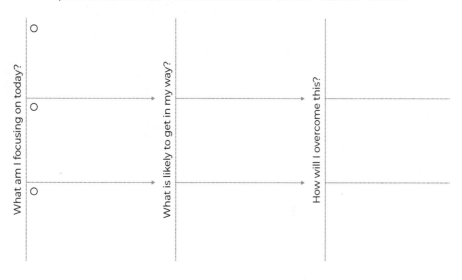

⊘ What will I say NO to today?

☾ DAILY REFLECTION

⟳ What's my favorite memory from today?

✔ Did I do what I said I would do?

What can I learn from this?

○ I reviewed my weekly tasks

♥ I am grateful for:

Because:

☀ HOW CAN I GET A LITTLE CLOSER TO MY GOALS TODAY?

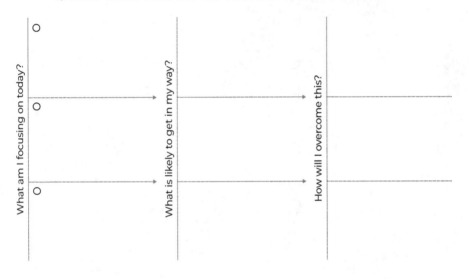

🚫 What will I say NO to today?

☾ DAILY REFLECTION

🕓 What's my favorite memory from today?

✅ Did I do what I said I would do?

What can I learn from this?

○ I reviewed my weekly tasks

♥ I am grateful for:

Because:

☀ HOW CAN I GET A LITTLE CLOSER TO MY GOALS TODAY?

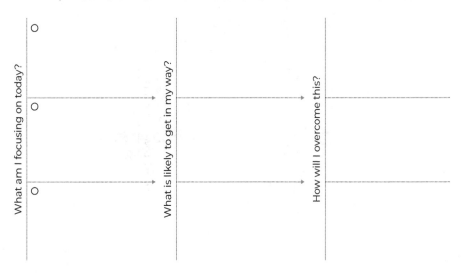

○ What will I say NO to today?

☾ DAILY REFLECTION

⟲ What's my favorite memory from today?

✔ Did I do what I said I would do?

What can I learn from this?

○ I reviewed my weekly tasks

♥ I am grateful for:

Because:

☀ HOW CAN I GET A LITTLE CLOSER TO MY GOALS TODAY?

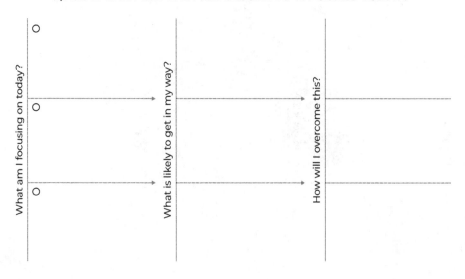

🚫 What will I say NO to today?

☾ DAILY REFLECTION

⟳ What's my favorite memory from today?

✔ Did I do what I said I would do?

What can I learn from this?

○ I reviewed my weekly tasks

♥ I am grateful for:

Because:

☀ HOW CAN I GET A LITTLE CLOSER TO MY GOALS TODAY?

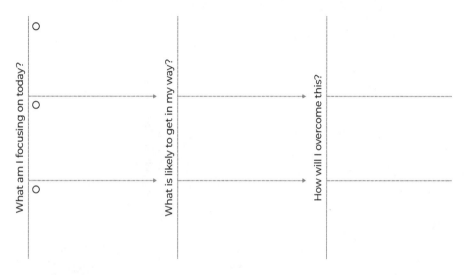

What am I focusing on today?

What is likely to get in my way?

How will I overcome this?

🚫 What will I say NO to today?

☾ DAILY REFLECTION

🕙 What's my favorite memory from today?

✔ Did I do what I said I would do?

What can I learn from this?

○ I reviewed my weekly tasks

♥ I am grateful for:

Because:

☀ HOW CAN I GET A LITTLE CLOSER TO MY GOALS TODAY?

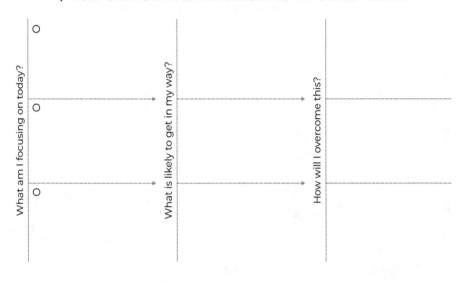

🚫 What will I say NO to today?

☾ DAILY REFLECTION

⟲ What's my favorite memory from today?

✔ Did I do what I said I would do?

What can I learn from this?

○ I reviewed my weekly tasks

♥ I am grateful for:

Because:

☀ HOW CAN I GET A LITTLE CLOSER TO MY GOALS TODAY?

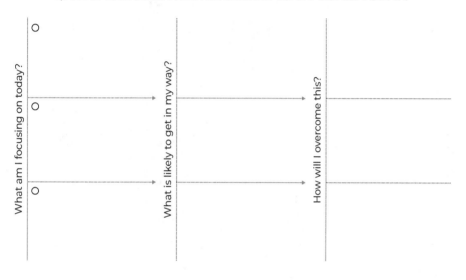

What am I focusing on today?

What is likely to get in my way?

How will I overcome this?

⊘ What will I say NO to today?

☾ DAILY REFLECTION

↺ What's my favorite memory from today?

✓ Did I do what I said I would do?

What can I learn from this?

○ I reviewed my weekly tasks

♥ I am grateful for:

Because:

☀ HOW CAN I GET A LITTLE CLOSER TO MY GOALS TODAY?

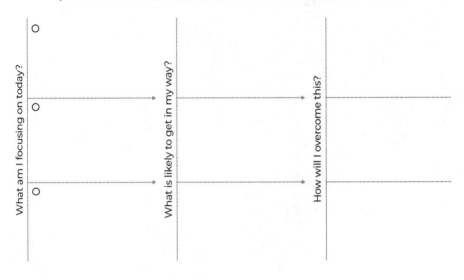

What am I focusing on today?

What is likely to get in my way?

How will I overcome this?

🚫 What will I say NO to today?

☾ DAILY REFLECTION

🕤 What's my favorite memory from today?

✅ Did I do what I said I would do?

What can I learn from this?

○ I reviewed my weekly tasks   **//ALIGNING TODAY** ..../........./...........

♥ I am grateful for:
Because:

☀ HOW CAN I GET A LITTLE CLOSER TO MY GOALS TODAY?

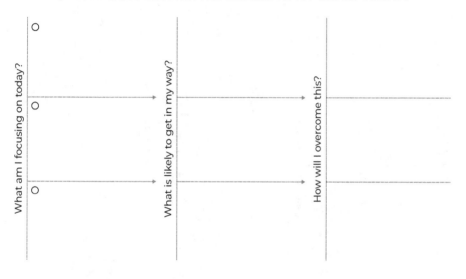

What am I focusing on today?

What is likely to get in my way?

How will I overcome this?

⊘ What will I say NO to today?

☾ DAILY REFLECTION

⟲ What's my favorite memory from today?

✔ Did I do what I said I would do?
What can I learn from this?

○ I reviewed my weekly tasks

♥ I am grateful for:

Because:

☀ HOW CAN I GET A LITTLE CLOSER TO MY GOALS TODAY?

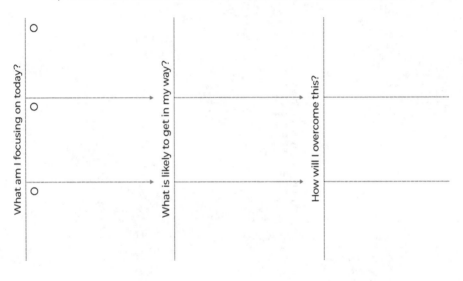

⊘ What will I say NO to today?

☾ DAILY REFLECTION

↻ What's my favorite memory from today?

✔ Did I do what I said I would do?

What can I learn from this?

○ I reviewed my weekly tasks

♥ I am grateful for:

Because:

☀ HOW CAN I GET A LITTLE CLOSER TO MY GOALS TODAY?

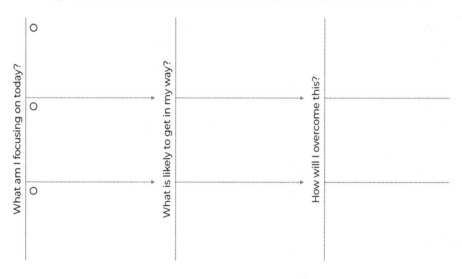

⊘ What will I say NO to today?

☾ DAILY REFLECTION

⟲ What's my favorite memory from today?

✔ Did I do what I said I would do?

What can I learn from this?

○ I reviewed my weekly tasks

♥ I am grateful for:

Because:

☀ HOW CAN I GET A LITTLE CLOSER TO MY GOALS TODAY?

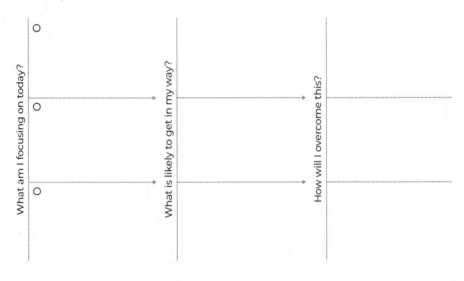

⊘ What will I say NO to today?

☾ DAILY REFLECTION

↺ What's my favorite memory from today?

✔ Did I do what I said I would do?

What can I learn from this?

○ I reviewed my weekly tasks

♥ I am grateful for:

Because:

☀ HOW CAN I GET A LITTLE CLOSER TO MY GOALS TODAY?

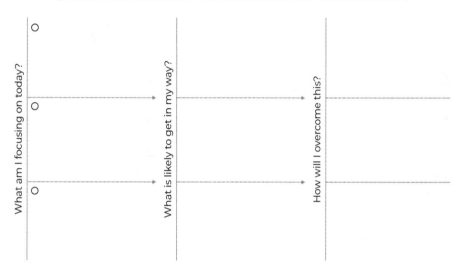

⊘ What will I say NO to today?

☾ DAILY REFLECTION

↺ What's my favorite memory from today?

✔ Did I do what I said I would do?

What can I learn from this?

♥ I am grateful for:

Because:

☀ HOW CAN I GET A LITTLE CLOSER TO MY GOALS TODAY?

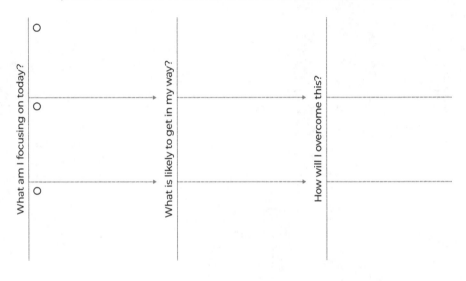

What am I focusing on today?

What is likely to get in my way?

How will I overcome this?

🚫 What will I say NO to today?

☾ DAILY REFLECTION

🔄 What's my favorite memory from today?

✔ Did I do what I said I would do?

What can I learn from this?

○ I reviewed my weekly tasks

♥ I am grateful for:

Because:

☀ HOW CAN I GET A LITTLE CLOSER TO MY GOALS TODAY?

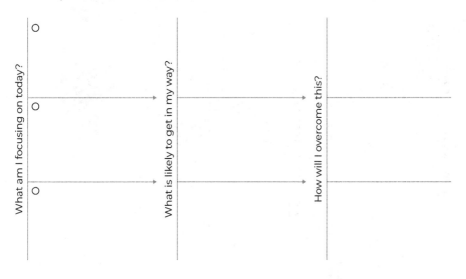

🚫 What will I say NO to today?

☾ DAILY REFLECTION

🕙 What's my favorite memory from today?

✅ Did I do what I said I would do?

What can I learn from this?

○ I reviewed my weekly tasks   **//ALIGNING TODAY** _____ / _____ / _____

♥ I am grateful for:

Because:

☀ HOW CAN I GET A LITTLE CLOSER TO MY GOALS TODAY?

○

○

○

What am I focusing on today?

What is likely to get in my way?

How will I overcome this?

⊘ What will I say NO to today?

☾ DAILY REFLECTION

⟲ What's my favorite memory from today?

✓ Did I do what I said I would do?

What can I learn from this?

○ I reviewed my weekly tasks

♥ I am grateful for:

Because:

☀ HOW CAN I GET A LITTLE CLOSER TO MY GOALS TODAY?

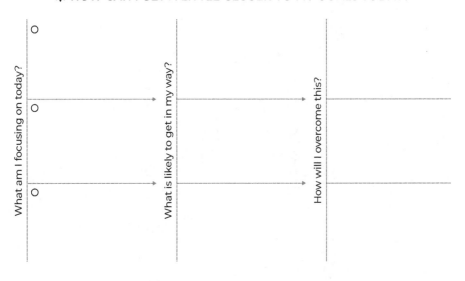

⊘ What will I say NO to today?

☾ DAILY REFLECTION

↻ What's my favorite memory from today?

✔ Did I do what I said I would do?

What can I learn from this?

○ I reviewed my weekly tasks   **//ALIGNING TODAY** ..../......../..........

♥ I am grateful for:

Because:

☼ HOW CAN I GET A LITTLE CLOSER TO MY GOALS TODAY?

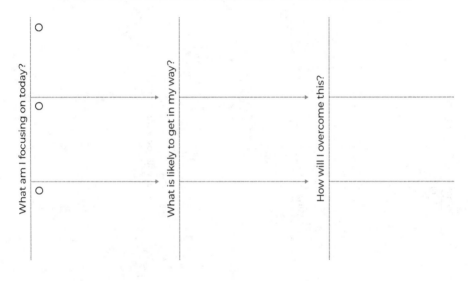

What am I focusing on today?

○

○

○

What is likely to get in my way?

How will I overcome this?

🚫 What will I say NO to today?

☾ DAILY REFLECTION

🕘 What's my favorite memory from today?

✔ Did I do what I said I would do?

What can I learn from this?

○ I reviewed my weekly tasks

♥ I am grateful for:

Because:

☼ HOW CAN I GET A LITTLE CLOSER TO MY GOALS TODAY?

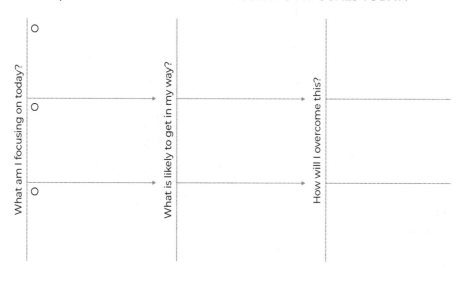

🚫 What will I say NO to today?

☾ DAILY REFLECTION

⟳ What's my favorite memory from today?

✔ Did I do what I said I would do?

What can I learn from this?

○ I reviewed my weekly tasks

♥ I am grateful for:

Because:

☀ HOW CAN I GET A LITTLE CLOSER TO MY GOALS TODAY?

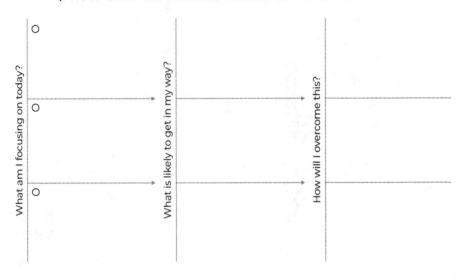

🚫 What will I say NO to today?

☾ DAILY REFLECTION

🕙 What's my favorite memory from today?

✔ Did I do what I said I would do?

What can I learn from this?

○ I reviewed my weekly tasks

♥ I am grateful for:

Because:

☀ HOW CAN I GET A LITTLE CLOSER TO MY GOALS TODAY?

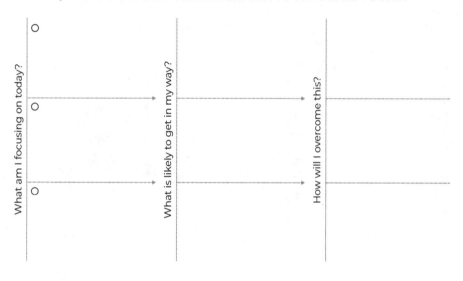

🚫 What will I say NO to today?

☾ DAILY REFLECTION

🕤 What's my favorite memory from today?

✔ Did I do what I said I would do?

What can I learn from this?

○ I reviewed my weekly tasks

♥ I am grateful for:

Because:

☀ HOW CAN I GET A LITTLE CLOSER TO MY GOALS TODAY?

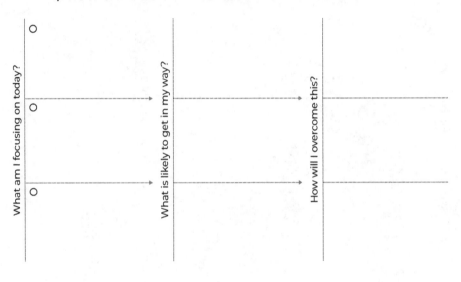

🚫 What will I say NO to today?

☾ DAILY REFLECTION

↻ What's my favorite memory from today?

✔ Did I do what I said I would do?

What can I learn from this?

○ I reviewed my weekly tasks

♥ I am grateful for:

Because:

☀ HOW CAN I GET A LITTLE CLOSER TO MY GOALS TODAY?

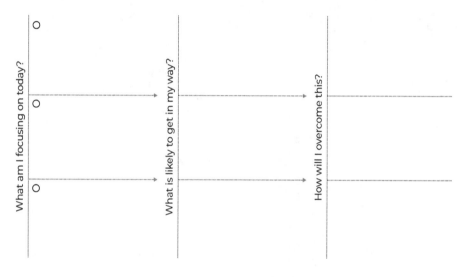

🚫 What will I say NO to today?

☾ DAILY REFLECTION

⟲ What's my favorite memory from today?

✔ Did I do what I said I would do?

What can I learn from this?

○ I reviewed my weekly tasks

♥ I am grateful for:

Because:

☀ HOW CAN I GET A LITTLE CLOSER TO MY GOALS TODAY?

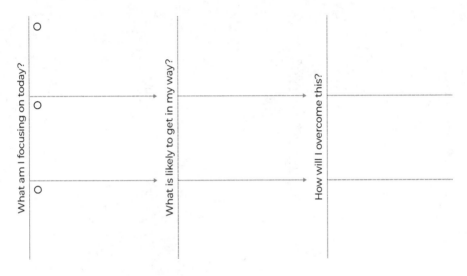

🚫 What will I say NO to today?

....

☾ DAILY REFLECTION

⟲ What's my favorite memory from today?

✔ Did I do what I said I would do?

What can I learn from this?

○ I reviewed my weekly tasks   **//ALIGNING TODAY** ..../........./...........

♥ I am grateful for:

Because:

☀ HOW CAN I GET A LITTLE CLOSER TO MY GOALS TODAY?

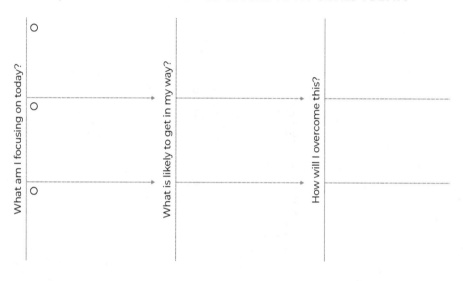

🚫 What will I say NO to today?

☾ DAILY REFLECTION

⟲ What's my favorite memory from today?

✔ Did I do what I said I would do?

What can I learn from this?

○ I reviewed my weekly tasks

♥ I am grateful for:

Because:

☼ HOW CAN I GET A LITTLE CLOSER TO MY GOALS TODAY?

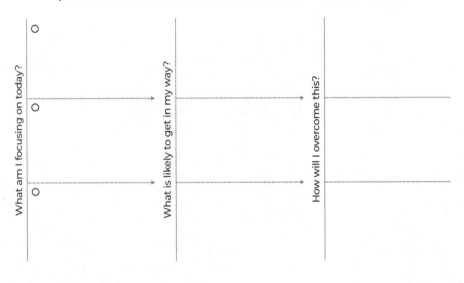

○

What am I focusing on today?

○

○

What is likely to get in my way?

How will I overcome this?

⊘ What will I say NO to today?

☾ DAILY REFLECTION

↺ What's my favorite memory from today?

✔ Did I do what I said I would do?

What can I learn from this?

○ I reviewed my weekly tasks

♥ I am grateful for:

Because:

☀ HOW CAN I GET A LITTLE CLOSER TO MY GOALS TODAY?

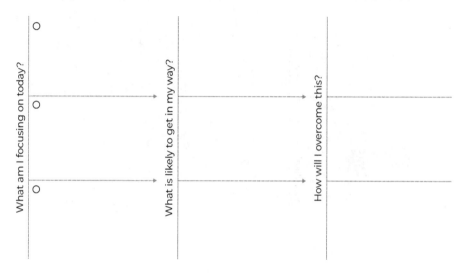

What am I focusing on today?

What is likely to get in my way?

How will I overcome this?

○ What will I say NO to today?

☾ DAILY REFLECTION

⟲ What's my favorite memory from today?

✔ Did I do what I said I would do?

What can I learn from this?

○ I reviewed my weekly tasks

♥ I am grateful for:

Because:

☼ HOW CAN I GET A LITTLE CLOSER TO MY GOALS TODAY?

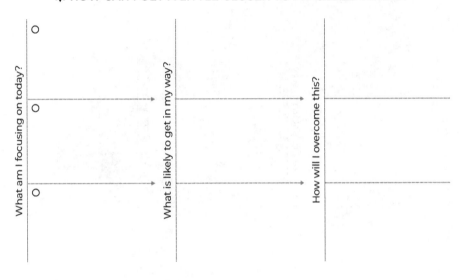

⊘ What will I say NO to today?

☾ DAILY REFLECTION

⟲ What's my favorite memory from today?

✔ Did I do what I said I would do?

What can I learn from this?

○ I reviewed my weekly tasks

♥ I am grateful for:

Because:

☀ HOW CAN I GET A LITTLE CLOSER TO MY GOALS TODAY?

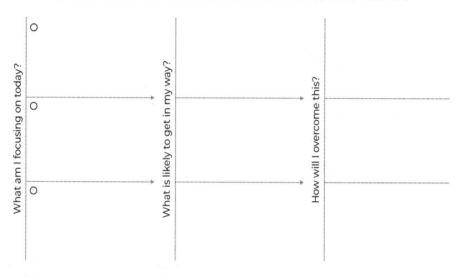

⃠ What will I say NO to today?

☾ DAILY REFLECTION

🕘 What's my favorite memory from today?

✔ Did I do what I said I would do?

What can I learn from this?

○ I reviewed my weekly tasks

♥ I am grateful for:

Because:

☀ HOW CAN I GET A LITTLE CLOSER TO MY GOALS TODAY?

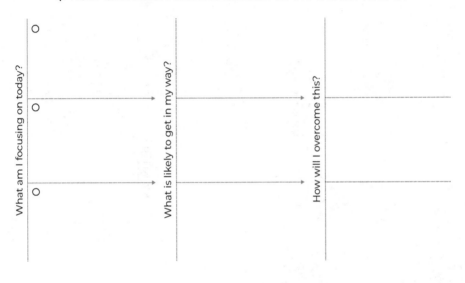

⊘ What will I say NO to today?

☾ DAILY REFLECTION

↺ What's my favorite memory from today?

✓ Did I do what I said I would do?

What can I learn from this?

○ I reviewed my weekly tasks

♥ I am grateful for:

Because:

☀ HOW CAN I GET A LITTLE CLOSER TO MY GOALS TODAY?

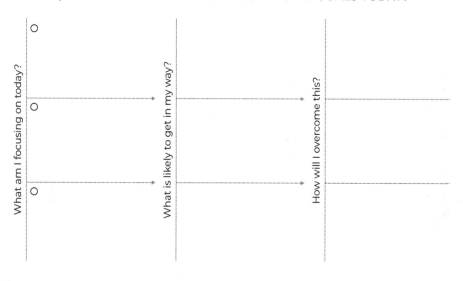

What am I focusing on today?

What is likely to get in my way?

How will I overcome this?

○
○
○

🚫 What will I say NO to today?

☾ DAILY REFLECTION

🕙 What's my favorite memory from today?

✓ Did I do what I said I would do?

What can I learn from this?

○ I reviewed my weekly tasks

♥ I am grateful for:

Because:

☀ HOW CAN I GET A LITTLE CLOSER TO MY GOALS TODAY?

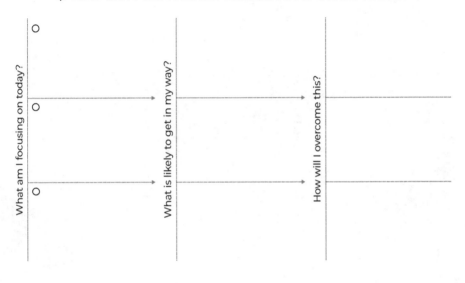

⊘ What will I say NO to today?

☾ DAILY REFLECTION

↺ What's my favorite memory from today?

✔ Did I do what I said I would do?

What can I learn from this?

○ I reviewed my weekly tasks

♥ I am grateful for:
Because:

☀ HOW CAN I GET A LITTLE CLOSER TO MY GOALS TODAY?

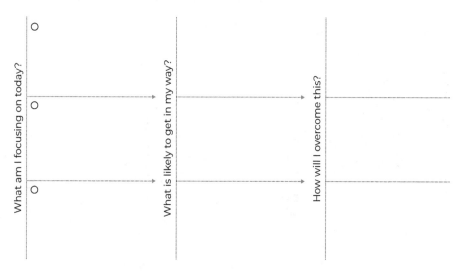

⊘ What will I say NO to today?

☾ DAILY REFLECTION

↺ What's my favorite memory from today?

✔ Did I do what I said I would do?
What can I learn from this?

○ I reviewed my weekly tasks

♥ I am grateful for:

Because:

☀ HOW CAN I GET A LITTLE CLOSER TO MY GOALS TODAY?

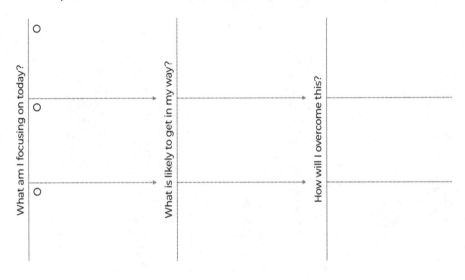

⊘ What will I say NO to today?

☾ DAILY REFLECTION

↻ What's my favorite memory from today?

✔ Did I do what I said I would do?

What can I learn from this?

○ I reviewed my weekly tasks

♥ I am grateful for:

Because:

☀ HOW CAN I GET A LITTLE CLOSER TO MY GOALS TODAY?

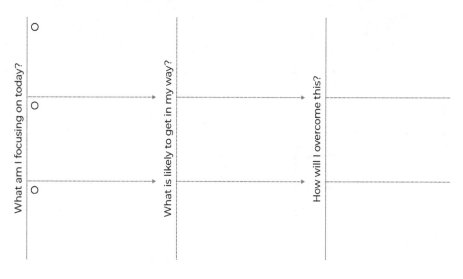

⊘ What will I say NO to today?

☾ DAILY REFLECTION

↻ What's my favorite memory from today?

✔ Did I do what I said I would do?

What can I learn from this?

○ I reviewed my weekly tasks

♥ I am grateful for:

Because:

☼ HOW CAN I GET A LITTLE CLOSER TO MY GOALS TODAY?

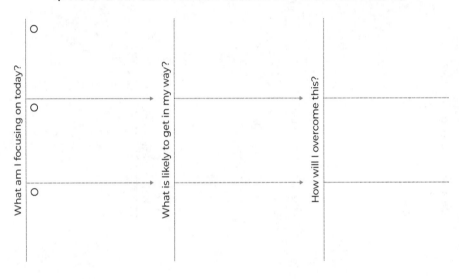

⊘ What will I say NO to today?

☾ DAILY REFLECTION

↻ What's my favorite memory from today?

✔ Did I do what I said I would do?

What can I learn from this?

○ I reviewed my weekly tasks **//ALIGNING TODAY** ..../........../..........

♥ I am grateful for:

Because:

☀ HOW CAN I GET A LITTLE CLOSER TO MY GOALS TODAY?

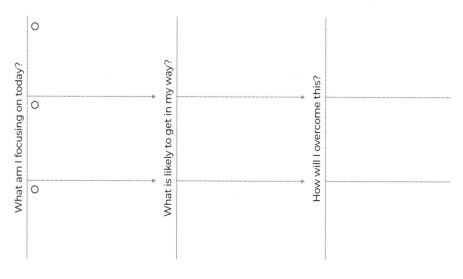

○

○

○

What am I focusing on today?

What is likely to get in my way?

How will I overcome this?

🚫 What will I say NO to today?

☾ DAILY REFLECTION

🕐 What's my favorite memory from today?

✔ Did I do what I said I would do?

What can I learn from this?

○ I reviewed my weekly tasks

♥ I am grateful for:

Because:

☀ HOW CAN I GET A LITTLE CLOSER TO MY GOALS TODAY?

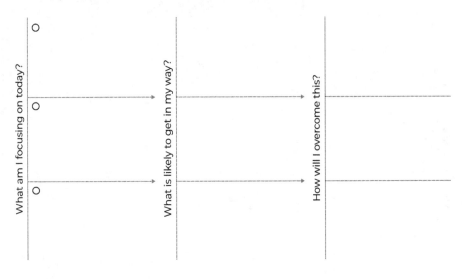

🚫 What will I say NO to today?

☾ DAILY REFLECTION

⟲ What's my favorite memory from today?

✔ Did I do what I said I would do?

What can I learn from this?

○ I reviewed my weekly tasks

♥ I am grateful for:

Because:

☼ HOW CAN I GET A LITTLE CLOSER TO MY GOALS TODAY?

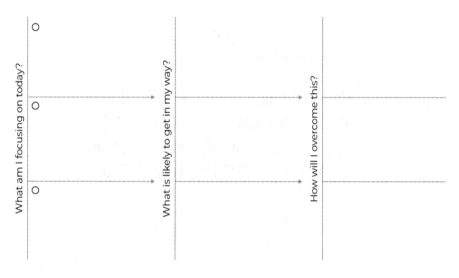

⊘ What will I say NO to today?

☾ DAILY REFLECTION

⟲ What's my favorite memory from today?

✔ Did I do what I said I would do?

What can I learn from this?

WHAT LIES BEHIND YOU
AND WHAT LIES IN FRONT OF
YOU, PALES IN COMPARISON
TO WHAT LIES INSIDE YOU.

—Ralph Waldo Emerson

REFLECT ON YOUR 90-DAY GOALS

ALIGNING YOUR TIME TO YOUR goals is a powerful, life-changing practice. You stuck with it all the way to the end! I'm impressed, and you should be, too.

Now it's time to look back, reflect, and learn.

♥ Savor the Good

The best part of using this journal just might very well be the record you now have of your favorite memories and gratitudes. Spend time savoring them as you reflect upon the last 90 days.

🥂 Celebrate Your Progress

You're moving in the right direction, and you are learning along the way. It's really easy to minimize your wins and focus on where you still have room to grow. Don't do that! Focus most of your energy on the progress you are making, as that's what creates momentum and gives you that warm feeling of satisfaction.

☺ Be Excited About Where You're Headed

No matter how much you improve, there will always be room to grow. This isn't a bad thing! How boring would life be if you had everything figured out? Well, no worries there! It's not possible. Instead, stay reflective, nimble, and experimental, and enjoy the ride.

🚶 Keep Going

This is just the beginning! The real magic happens when aligning your time to your goals becomes a way of life. Grab your next Aligned Time Journal, and let's plan for the next 90-days!

🕘 **My favorite memories from the past 90 days are:**

1	2	3
3	4	5

How did I do against my goals? Did I do them? What can I learn from this?

◎ **Stretch Goal:**

Learning:

◎ **Support Goal:**

Learning:

◎ **Sanity Goal:**

Learning:

💡 **What did I learn about myself as I pursued these goals?**

90-DAY REFLECTION: WEB OF LIFE

USING THE SAME CIRCLES YOU used during your 90-day planning, re-assess your Web of Life. **Remember:**

1. **Mark how satisfied you are in this area of your life** by placing a dot on the line between the word "low" and the circle. The closer to the word "low," the less satisfied you are. Connect the dots with a line to see your web of satisfaction.

2. **Rank order them from 1-12 according to their priority to you.** On the line next to each circle, give each area a rank order. Force yourself to choose between items that feel identical in their priority to you.

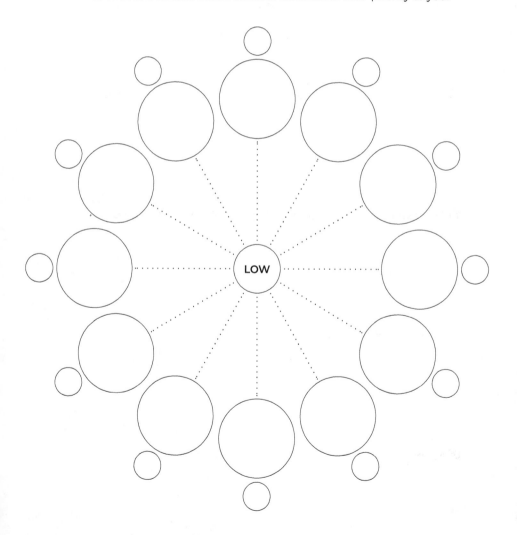

Now, look at your updated Web of Life and notice what you notice.

📈 Did I have the impact I was hoping for?

📌 What still needs some attention?

☺ When I was at my best in the past 90 days, what words described me?

➲ What were my biggest breakthroughs from the past 90 days?

♥ For what am I most grateful from the past 90 days?

🔖 As I begin the next 90 days, what am I keeping in mind?